*JUST COMMAS

9 BASIC RULES TO MASTER COMMA USAGE

DIANE LUTOVICH & JANIS FISHER CHAN

Advanced Communication Designs Inc.

San Anselmo, California

Design and typography: Christi Payne, Book Arts

Acknowledgements:

Century Handbook of Writing, Garland Greever and Easley S. Jones. The Century Company, New York, 1918.

English the Easy Way, Harriet Diamond (Contributor) and Phyllis Dutwin (Contributor). Barrons Educational Series, 1996.

The King's English, H.W. Fowler and F. G. Fowler. Oxford University Press, 1930.

For information:

Advanced Communication Designs, Inc.
P.O. Box 2504, San Anselmo, CA 94979
Phone: 415-459-3563   Fax: 415-459-8618
Email: adcom@linex.com
On the Web: **www.writeitwell.com**

ISBN: 0-9637455-6-5

*JUST COMMAS

9 BASIC RULES TO MASTER COMMA USAGE

The comma . . . has not one but many tasks to do, which differ greatly in importance.

THE KING'S ENGLISH, 1930.

Introduction _____

There is nothing straightforward about the rules of comma use in the English language. For one thing, the comma serves many different purposes, and for another, it is the most widely used of all punctuation marks. Not surprising, then, that the comma is also the most troublesome. In fact, its overuse and misuse obscure meaning more than the faulty usage of any other mark.

The purpose of commas is not to confuse writers, but to help readers. Commas keep sentence parts from bumping into each other, causing confusion, misreadings, and mistakes. In fact, what we're trying to do for the comma is what the comma tries to do for the written language—make things clear.

Everyone who has studied the language has been taught how to use commas not once, but many times. In fact, in the hundreds of writing workshops we have taught over the years, the most frequently asked questions concern commas. That is why we wrote *Just Commas,* a book with just one mission—to clear up, once and for all, comma confusion.

How to Use This Book

▶ Pay close attention to "Common Comma Blunders." In most cases, they represent the confusion that comes from too many conflicting voices—your English teacher, the person who sat next to you in composition, even your parents.

▶ Try the practice exercises. They'll give you a good idea of whether you're learning the rules or need to go back and repeat a section.

▶ Keep this book for reference. You don't have to memorize all the rules. Even professional writers look things up when they aren't sure.

▶ *Just Commas* focuses on the most frequent uses of the comma. It does not attempt to cover every rule or address every situation in which you might wonder how to use commas. But the book comes with an on-line help service through our web site: **www.writeitwell.com**. We will do our best to answer your questions.

Turn the page for an overview of the rules covered in this book.

If three people applied for a position and all were equally qualified, I would choose the one who used commas correctly. It would tell me a lot about what that person thought was important.

HUMAN RESOURCES DIRECTOR

The Rules _____

Rule 1. **USE COMMAS TO SEPARATE ITEMS IN A SERIES (*Page 11*)**

The conference activities included seminars on marketing, workshops on newsletter design, and preparation for a sales campaign.

Welcome to a world of service and amenities that include three magnificent beaches, five restaurants, an oceanside tennis garden, spa facilities, and 36 holes of golf.

Rule 2. **USE COMMAS WHEN JOINING TWO INDEPENDENT CLAUSES WITH A COORDINATING CONJUNCTION (*Page 17*)**

Impressionists saw nature as color swimming in light, and they provided people with a new way to compare nature and art.

Both Greek and Latin classical writers took an interest in Egypt, and their manuscripts have been preserved in Rome and in Byzantium.

For more on the independent clause and coordinating conjunctions, see pages 8 and 9.

Rule 3. ***USE COMMAS TO SEPARATE INTRODUCTORY WORDS FROM THE REST OF THE SENTENCE (Page 27)***

After declaring he would not move to another office, Alexander changed his mind when he saw the view he would have of the Golden Gate Bridge.

Each time the lobster expands from within, the confining shell must be sloughed off.

Rule 4. ***USE COMMAS TO SET OFF WORD GROUPS THAT ARE NOT ESSENTIAL TO THE MEANING OF THE SENTENCE (Page 31)***

Poetry, like history and science, is a way of using language.

The Mississippi River, the longest river in the United States, is three miles wide when it empties into the Gulf of Mexico.

Rule 5. ***USE COMMAS TO SET OFF CERTAIN TRANSITIONAL EXPRESSIONS AND CONTRASTING STATEMENTS (Page 39)***

We are very pleased, however, with the results of our new marketing effort.

I asked you to send a shipment of shirts, not pants.

| Rule 6. | ***USE COMMAS BETWEEN ADJECTIVES THAT CAN BE REARRANGED WITHOUT CHANGING THE MEANING (Page 53)*** |

Prepare to review the new, exciting, controversial magazine we're publishing next month.

The foundation is seeking an efficient, critical, well-organized, energetic person to replace the retiring director.

| Rule 7. | ***USE COMMAS TO SET OFF DIRECT QUOTATIONS (Page 59)*** |

Project Manager Sue Chung explained, "We need to choose a new committee because the current members are all being transferred to Idaho."

In speaking to the audience, the famous author begged, "Please forgive me for playing a tape of my reading, but my voice is almost gone."

Rule 8. USE COMMAS TO SEPARATE THE PARTS OF DATES, ADDRESSES, AND NUMBERS *(Page 67)*

As of June 1, 2000, my address will be 2110 Sixth Avenue East, Hibbing, MN 55126.

The chamber group's only local performance will be held in the Civic Center Auditorium, 462 San Pablo Drive, Room 23, Maple Grove, at 2:30 p.m., Sunday, March 1, 2000.

Rule 9. USE COMMAS TO SET OFF OTHER PUNCTUATION MARKS *(Page 73)*

The campground offers many choices of outdoor recreation (which most of you listed as a high priority), and all activities are included in the fee.

Please make an appointment with Jolene Finetti, M.D., to discuss alternative therapies.

To use commas correctly, you have to be able to recognize an independent clause, a subject, and a coordinating conjunction. If you remember what they are, you can skip this section; if not, review them now.

INDEPENDENT CLAUSE.   A group of words that could stand on its own as a complete sentence.

The following sentence has two independent clauses, joined with "and" and a comma:

(1) Pete received the honor in his department for selling the most advertising space, <u>and</u> (2) he plans on doing even better next year.

SUBJECT.   Who or what the sentence is about. Each independent clause needs at least one subject.

There are two subjects in this sentence, one in each independent clause:

<u>Pete</u> received the honor in his department for selling the most advertising space, and <u>he</u> plans on doing even better next year.

COORDINATING CONJUNCTION.   Words that connect the parts of a sentence and show the relationship between words and ideas. There are seven commonly used coordinating conjunctions in English: **but, and, for, nor, or, so,** and **yet.**

This sentence has two coordinating conjunctions:

Simple gifts are usually the best, <u>but</u> it's not always easy to find the right gift for the occasion, <u>and</u> I sometimes end up buying one that's too expensive.

Rules are made to be broken —but when you break them, be willing to sweep up the pieces

JASON FALKE

Rule 1

USE COMMAS TO SEPARATE ITEMS IN A SERIES

 *Think About It*

Without commas, items in a series can run into each other. Commas make it clear that each item in the series is a separate item.

Without commas | Preparing for the sailing expedition meant purchasing and learning to use a G.P.S. becoming familiar with the short-wave radio making sure the water purifier was working and studying all available harbor maps.

With commas | Preparing for the sailing expedition meant purchasing and learning to use a G.P.S., becoming familiar with the short-wave radio, making sure the water purifier was working, and studying all available harbor maps.

The most common question about using commas in a series is whether to use a comma before the "and." In fact, there is no hard and fast rule about that comma (sometimes called the "series" comma).

▶ Always use the series comma if the sentence might be confusing without it. In the following example, it's hard to tell which tasks go together. See how the series comma before the final "and" clears up the confusion.

Without series comma The tasks we must complete by next Wednesday include filing our tax return, making sure there is enough money in the bank to cover the check and the loan payment and making our IRA contribution.

With series comma The tasks we must complete by next Wednesday include filing our tax return, making sure there is enough money in the bank to cover the check and the loan payment, and making our IRA contribution.

▶ You may use the series comma or leave it out when the series contains only a few simple items.

Series comma optional We plan to hire a programmer, a receptionist, a personnel manager(,) and three administrative assistants.

If you don't want to stop and think about whether to use a comma before the last item in the series, use it all the time. You won't be wrong.

▶ Using a comma before the first item in the series.

Wrong I plan to make, seven copies of the report, send one to each of the directors, and bind the seventh copy.

Right I plan to make seven copies of the report, send one to each of the directors, and bind the seventh copy.

▶ Using a comma after the "and" in a series.

Wrong Send our Human Resource Department your application, a resume and, three letters of reference.

Right Send our Human Resource Department your application, a resume, and three letters of reference.

Examples

In the following examples, the optional commas are circled.

Wrong   Jon asked Aaron, to clean the shelves, organize the books in alphabetical order, and send all duplicate copies to the warehouse.

Right   Jon asked Aaron to clean the shelves, organize the books in alphabetical order(,) and send all duplicate copies to the warehouse.

Wrong   Open your account with our bank by June 1st to receive free checks, an ATM card good anywhere in the world and, a subscription to our monthly travel magazine.

Right   Open your account with our bank by June 1st to receive free checks, an ATM card good anywhere in the world(,) and a subscription to our monthly travel magazine.

Confusing   The activities included seminars on marketing, workshops on newsletter design and promotion and preparation for a sales campaign.

Clear   The activities included seminars on marketing, workshops on newsletter design and promotion, and preparation for a sales campaign.

And it must be added that nothing so easily exposes a writer to the suspicion of being uneducated as omission of commas against nearly universal custom. The King's English, 1930.

USE COMMAS WHEN JOINING TWO INDEPENDENT CLAUSES WITH A COORDINATING CONJUNCTION

Think About It

A comma, like a weak trailer hitch, is not strong enough to connect two separate independent clauses—unless you also use a coordinating conjunction. Two kinds of errors can result from failing to join two independent clauses correctly.

A **comma splice** is what you get when you use a comma to join two independent clauses without the coordinating conjunction. This kind of problem is usually the result of failing to recognize that the sentence contains two independent clauses.

You get a **run-on sentence** when you join two independent clauses without using either a coordinating conjunction or a comma. This kind of writing error is usually the result of carelessness.

Comma splice	The electrician needs access to the roof, please have someone available to unlock the door.
Run-on sentence	The electrician needs access to the roof please have someone available to unlock the door.
Sentence repaired	The electrician needs access to the roof, so please have someone available to unlock the door.

▶ You always need a coordinating conjunction to join two independent clauses, and it's never wrong to include a comma. You can leave the comma out if the clauses are short and closely related, but it's helpful to readers if you use a comma to separate clauses that are more than one line long.

Comma optional	Everyone in the group played guitar‚but only Dylan insisted that his friends listen to him.
Comma helpful	We can anticipate changes and prepare for them even as we try to prevent them, but the aging process is as inevitable for an oak tree as it is for each one of us.

Keep in mind that an independent clause can stand on its own as a complete sentence. When you join two independent clauses with a coordinating conjunction, you are actually joining two sentences.

▶ Using a comma to separate a group of words from its subject.

The manager is the only subject in the sentence below, and the subject appears only once, in the independent clause. If you use a comma to separate the words "is aware of all problems" from the first part of the sentence, you create a sentence fragment that has no subject.

Wrong A good <u>manager</u> knows the status of every project, and is aware of all problems.

Right A good <u>manager</u> knows the status of every project and is aware of all problems.

▶ Putting the comma after the coordinating conjunction instead of before it.

Wrong Italians have been practicing artichoke cultivation for at least two thousand years and, they have a more highly developed expertise in its use than most Americans.

Right Italians have been practicing artichoke cultivation for at least two thousand years, and they have a more highly developed expertise in its use than most Americans.

Examples

In the following examples, the optional commas are circled.

Wrong   Several galleries show my grandmother's paintings, and sell several of them each year.

Right   Several galleries show my grandmother's paintings and sell several of them each year.

Wrong   I am staring at the mast, and see that the black line of a crack is clearly visible in the gray paint.

Right   I am staring at the mast and see that the black line of a crack is clearly visible in the gray paint.

Wrong   Charlene was disappointed when she failed to win the lottery but, she told everyone that she would be back next week.

Right   Charlene was disappointed when she failed to win the lottery, but she told everyone that she would be back next week.

Try It

Insert commas as needed in these sentences.

1. Companies need good job descriptions and standards output goals and measurement devices and regular feedback and review to make any monitoring system work but they must also make sure employees have adequate training.

2. The mortgage broker told Vanitha to sign all applicable releases and he asked her to submit two years' tax returns two recent bank statements and a copy of her most recent pay stub.

3. Yasha purchased some Russian videos on his last trip to Moscow and played them over and over for his bored friends.

4. Ella wanted to serve as president of the Poetry Center but she was afraid she would have too little time to work on her poetry.

5. Too many politicians say whatever people want to hear but seldom honor their commitments.

6. The caterers the event organizers selected for the anniversary party came highly recommended by people we trust so we are confident that the food will be excellent.

Check your answers on the next page.

The optional commas are circled. If you missed any, review the pages shown in parentheses.

1. Companies need good job descriptions and standards, output goals and measurement devices, and regular feedback and review to make any monitoring system work, but they must also make sure employees have adequate training. *(Page 12)*

2. The mortgage broker told Vanitha to sign all applicable releases, and he asked her to submit two year's tax returns, two recent bank statements(,) and a copy of her most recent pay stub. *(Pages 12 and 18)*

3. Yasha purchased some Russian videos on his last trip to Moscow and played them over and over for his bored friends. *(Page 20)*

4. Ella wanted to serve as president of the Poetry Center(,) but she was afraid she would have too little time to work on her poetry. *(Page 18)*

5. Too many politicians say whatever people want to hear but seldom honor their commitments. *(Page 20)*

6. The caterers the event organizers selected for the anniversary party came highly recommended by people we trust⊙so we are confident that the food will be excellent. *(Page 18)*

For a quick check on whether to use a comma, underline the subject or subjects in the sentence. Then be careful not to put in a comma that would separate a group of words from its subject.

Punctuation is used in writing as gestures, pauses, and changes of voice are used in speaking—to add force or to reveal the precise relationship of thoughts. In minor details of punctuation there is room for individual preference, but in essential principles all trustworthy writers agree.

CENTURY HANDBOOK OF WRITING, 1918

Rule 3

USE COMMAS TO SEPARATE INTRODUCTORY WORDS FROM THE REST OF THE SENTENCE

Think About It

Many sentences begin with a group of words that introduce the main point. These word groups usually tell when, where, how, why, or under what conditions the main action of the sentence takes place.

A comma tells readers that the introductory clause or phrase has come to a close and the main part of the sentence is about to begin. These words are like "The Star-Spangled Banner," which prepares baseball players and fans for the main event.

This comma serves two purposes:

▶ It keeps the introductory words from running into the main part of the sentence, thus preventing misreadings.

Confusing   If Sue files Jim will deliver the proposals.

Clear   If Sue files, Jim will deliver the proposals.

- ▶ It provides a brief pause before the reader plunges into the main point of the sentence. The comma is especially useful if the introductory clause is a long one. You can leave it out if the introductory clause is short and there's no danger of confusion.

Confusing   After working closely with her attorney to get the brief to Judge Jaffe by the first of May April realized she wanted to call off the trial while there was still time.

Clear   After working closely with her attorney to get the brief to Judge Jaffe by the first of May**,** April realized she wanted to call off the trial while there was still time.

Confusing   When Claude had finished packing his clothes were so wrinkled he couldn't wear them.

Clear   When Claude had finished packing**,** his clothes were so wrinkled he couldn't wear them.

Comma optional   After opening the new office**(,)** the CEO took the staff on a cruise to show her appreciation for their hard work.

Common Comma Blunder

▶ Using a comma after the subject instead of the introductory clause.

Wrong   While Cyrus was preparing his gourmet dinner his guests, telephoned to say they would not be coming.

Right   While Cyrus was preparing his gourmet dinner, his guests telephoned to say they would not be coming.

Wrong   Three days before Maria left on her year-long sabbatical her brother, called to say he had found a tenant to sublet her apartment.

Right   Three days before Maria left on her year-long sabbatical, her brother called to say he had found a tenant to sublet her apartment.

29

Examples

Confusing   If the Foundation President retires her project manager will leave at the same time.

Clear   If the Foundation President retires, her project manager will leave at the same time.

Confusing   Geographically closer to Atlanta than Miami Tallahassee is much more like a traditional southern city than its neighbors to the south.

Clear   Geographically closer to Atlanta than Miami, Tallahassee is much more like a traditional southern city than its neighbors to the south.

Comma optional   Convinced that all the information in the report was accurate, the consultant submitted it to her client.

Comma optional   As a black hole emits particles, its mass and size steadily decrease.

Comma optional   After carefully selecting his new computer, Justin was still disappointed once he got it home.

USE COMMAS TO SET OFF WORD GROUPS THAT ARE NOT ESSENTIAL TO THE MEANING OF THE SENTENCE

Think About It

Use commas to set off words that add nonessential information to a sentence. Words are nonessential if they can be removed without changing the meaning of the sentence.

The wine country, a popular tourist destination, is less than an hour by car from San Francisco.

The wine country is less than an hour by car from San Francisco.

Nonessential word groups include:

▶ Words that stand for—or name—the noun or noun phrase that immediately precedes them. (These words are called "appositives.") Notice that the essential meaning of the following sentences does not change if the underlined words are removed.

My brother, <u>John Sampson</u>, is a foreman at the new construction firm, <u>J.S. Lewis Associates</u>.

My brother is a foreman at the new construction firm.

Your home town, <u>San Francisco</u>, tops the list of prospective locations for our new store.

Your home town tops the list of prospective locations for our new store.

▶ Words that are purely descriptive or simply serve to give readers more information.

We decided to buy the house, <u>which had been neglected for years</u>, because we fell in love with the view.

We decided to buy the house because we fell in love with the view.

This course, <u>designed for amateur gardeners</u>, focuses on environmentally safe ways to combat garden pests.

This course focuses on environmentally safe ways to combat garden pests.

▶ Words added to a sentence for emphasis, if those words can be removed without changing the meaning.

Yes, I will consider you carefully for the office manager position as soon as I get an okay from Perry.

I will consider you carefully for the office manager position as soon as I get an okay from Perry.

Sorah is, not surprisingly, an excellent chemist, and I believe, Sam, we should find a way to provide her with her own lab.

Sorah is an excellent chemist, and I believe we should find a way to provide her with her own lab.

Here's a quick check: Write the sentence without the words you think can be removed. If the essential meaning of the sentence changes, don't use commas.

▶ Setting off essential information with commas.
In these examples, removing the underlined words changes the meaning of the sentence, so you would not set them off with commas.

All doctors <u>new</u> <u>to</u> <u>the</u> <u>staff</u> should plan on attending the retreat next Friday.

All doctors should plan on attending the retreat next Friday.

All automobiles <u>that</u> <u>were</u> <u>designed</u> <u>before</u> <u>1935</u> are eligible to participate in the parade.

All automobiles are eligible to participate in the parade.

▶ Leaving out the first or second comma of a pair.
When the nonessential words come in the middle of a sentence, always use a pair of commas, one at the beginning of the group of words and one at the end.

Wrong   The conference features Paul Landis, the well-known training consultant as keynote speaker.

Right   The conference features Paul Landis, the well-known training consultant, as keynote speaker.

Wrong   The apartment which we had rented through the Internet, proved to be surprisingly spacious and comfortable.

Right   The apartment, which we had rented through the Internet, proved to be surprisingly spacious and comfortable.

Wrong   John Steinbeck's classic novel of the Depression *The Grapes of Wrath* is still being read in schools.

Right   John Steinbeck's classic novel of the Depression, *The Grapes of Wrath,* is still being read in schools.

Wrong   The entrance exam, that was offered to all recent graduates, was very challenging.

Right   The entrance exam that was offered to all recent graduates was very challenging.

Wrong   I know spring is here when my fruit trees which I planted myself, begin to bloom.

Right   I know spring is here when my fruit trees, which I planted myself, begin to bloom.

Wrong   Our new product line which has been in development for three years will be previewed at the September meeting.

Right   Our new product line, which has been in development for three years, will be previewed at the September meeting.

Wrong   No I don't think it is wise to open a new branch at this time.

Right   No, I don't think it is wise to open a new branch at this time.

Wrong   A well-known local celebrity, a person whose name you would immediately recognize has agreed to host the charity auction this year.

Right   A well-known local celebrity, a person whose name you would immediately recognize, has agreed to host the charity auction this year.

Wrong   One of my favorite actors Sarah Light is terrific in her newest movie.

Right   One of my favorite actors, Sarah Light, is terrific in her newest movie.

If a sentence seems to call for too many commas and you're not sure where to place them, consider rewriting the sentence.

PROFESSOR JEFFERY CHAN

Rule 5

USE COMMAS TO SET OFF CERTAIN TRANSITIONAL EXPRESSIONS AND CONTRASTING STATEMENTS

Think About It

This rule covers words that show the relationship between thoughts and those that contrast one idea with another. You almost always set these kinds of words and word groups off with commas.

Transitional expressions help readers understand the logical relationship between sentences and parts of sentences. They can also be used for emphasis.

The university offers a wide range of Saturday morning language classes. For example, next semester you could take the first level of Italian, Farsi, or Mandarin.

We hope you will accept our offer. If you feel you must decline, however, please let us know right away.

Her father advised Tracy to invest in a mutual fund. Nevertheless, she used all her savings to buy a mini-van so she could carry her racing bicycle to competitions.

Here are some common transitional expressions:

however	moreover	therefore
meanwhile	nevertheless	for example
in fact	indeed	after all
in addition	as a result	finally
as a matter of fact	thus	in other words
on the other hand	at the same time	as you know
at any rate	also	perhaps

Contrasting statements usually begin with a word such as "not" or "unlike."

Georgia, unlike her brother, continued to play the viola.

Now that Paula had her degree, her manager talked to her as a professional, not as a subordinate.

Ramon purchased a compact car, unlike his friends who were buying trucks.

Here are guidelines for using commas with transitional expressions and contrasting statements.

▶ Place a comma after a transitional expression or contrasting statement that begins a sentence.

As you know, the loan is currently being refinanced.

On the other hand, we agree with the decision to begin construction in May.

Meanwhile, our review committee will consider your most recent manuscript.

Unlike her old desk, Jane's new one had space for all of her supplies.

Not only did Jory enter the race, she placed in the top ten runners for her age group.

▶ Place commas before and after transitional expressions and contrasting statements that come in the middle of a sentence.

The new brochure, moreover, can be slipped into an envelope.

The final report, nevertheless, covers all the important issues we discussed.

Hal's commitment, on the other hand, is sincere.

Poetry, unlike prose, uses as few words as possible to describe a sunset.

Women soccer players, unlike women softball players, have started to attract media attention.

The Peterson Company, not the Seascape Institute, won first place in the design competition.

▶ Place a comma before a transitional expression or contrasting statement that ends a sentence.

Time often plays tricks, for example.

We were meaning to call next week about your vacation rental, as a matter of fact.

Parsons continues to favor a conservative investment strategy, as you know.

The most recent building plans call for 30 parking spaces, not the 50 originally planned.

Peter excelled in sports, unlike his brother.

▶ Transitional expressions that fit very smoothly into a sentence may not need to be set off with commas. For example, in the following sentences, the commas may be left out or added for emphasis.

Right The shipment will arrive late and therefore must be inventoried immediately.

Right The shipment will arrive late and, therefore, must be inventoried immediately.

Right   As a result we will be unable to complete the project by the deadline.

Right   As a result, we will be unable to complete the project by the deadline.

▶ Setting transitional words off with commas if removing them calls for an unnecessary pause that makes a subtle change in the meaning.

Wrong Perhaps, we can meet for lunch next week to discuss the proposal in some detail.

Right Perhaps we can meet for lunch next week to discuss the proposal in some detail.

Wrong Certain wines from California's Central Valley are, also, selling well in the world market.

Right Certain wines from California's Central Valley are also selling well in the world market.

▶ Leaving out the first or second comma of a pair. When the transitional word or expression or contrasted element comes in the middle of a sentence, always use a pair of commas, one before the word or group of words, and one at the end.

Wrong The deposition, however took three hours longer than we had expected.

Right The deposition, however, took three hours longer than we had expected.

Wrong	Jayne's new position, unlike her former one provides her with a liberal expense account.
Right	Jayne's new position, unlike her former one, provides her with a liberal expense account.
Wrong	Sitting for an hour watching clouds move across the sky is in my opinion, a valuable use of time.
Right	Sitting for an hour watching clouds move across the sky is, in my opinion, a valuable use of time.

Wrong   The accident rate, furthermore has declined by nearly ten per cent over the past year.

Right   The accident rate, furthermore, has declined by nearly ten per cent over the past year.

Wrong   Although, learning another language is not essential for success, it can broaden your understanding of other cultures.

Right   Although learning another language is not essential for success, it can broaden your understanding of other cultures.

Wrong   I will however be out of town the week you plan to visit our offices.

Right   I will, however, be out of town the week you plan to visit our offices.

Wrong   The conference will be held in Phoenix not in Honolulu.

Right   The conference will be held in Phoenix, not in Honolulu.

Some authors would seem to have an occasional feeling that here or hereabouts is the place for a comma, just as in handwriting some persons are well content if they get a dot in somewhere within measurable distance of its I. The dot is generally over the right word at any rate, and the comma is seldom more than one word off its true place.

THE KING'S ENGLISH, 1930

Insert commas as needed in these sentences.

1. Slipping quietly into his seat Jason hoped that no one would notice he had missed the first 30 minutes of the demonstration.

2. Georgia's new boots which she bought after months of searching caused huge blisters the first time she wore them.

3. Jeff's father they say was a hard-working man.

4. Theresa is therefore going to apply for the new position not the one she had thought would be perfect for her.

5. The new format for example required such small print that not everyone could read it.

6. If you still think it is your job to photocopy Tomas will be very relieved.

7. The customers who want to preview our new products may attend next month's trade show as our guests.

8. Deciding that no response was the best response Arturo who was usually the first to speak up remained silent after all.

9. As a matter of fact I visited a new restaurant that would be ideal for your parents' anniversary party.

10. When you have an overnight package to ship the mail room staff needs it before noon.

11. I understand that our new research and development director Tom Leung is a former classmate of yours from Yale.

12. Shawn ordered the flowers to be delivered on Sue's birthday not the following day.

Answers

The optional commas are circled. If you missed any, review the pages shown in parentheses.

1. Slipping quietly into his seat(,) Jason hoped that no one would notice he had missed the first 30 minutes of the demonstration. *(Pages 27 and 28)*

2. Georgia's new boots, which she bought after months of searching, caused huge blisters the first time she wore them. *(Page 32)*

3. Jeff's father, they say, was a hard-working man. *(Page 41)*

4. Theresa is, therefore, going to apply for the new position, not the one she had thought would be perfect for her. *(Pages 41 and 42)*

5. The new format, for example, required such small print that not everyone could read it. *(Page 41)*

6. If you still think it is your job to photocopy, Tomas will be very relieved. *(Page 27)*

7. The customers who want to preview our new products may attend next month's trade show as our guests. *(Page 34)*

8. Deciding that no response was the best response, Arturo, who was usually the first to speak up, remained silent after all. *(Pages 27, 28, and 32)*

9. As a matter of fact, I visited a new restaurant that would be ideal for your parents' anniversary party. *(Page 40)*

10. When you have an overnight package to ship, the mail room staff needs it before noon. *(Page 27)*

11. I understand that our new research and development director, Tom Leung, is a former classmate of yours from Yale. *(Pages 31 and 32)*

12. Shawn ordered the flowers to be delivered on Sue's birthday, not the following day. *(Page 42)*

Do not sprinkle commas when the sentence is moving along freely with no complications in the thought.

THE CENTURY HANDBOOK OF WRITING, 1918.

Rule 6 _____

USE COMMAS BETWEEN ADJECTIVES THAT CAN BE REARRANGED WITHOUT CHANGING THE MEANING

Think About It

Adjectives are words that tell us something about a noun.

The <u>hot</u> fire warmed Cassandra quickly after her <u>brisk</u> walk in the <u>icy</u> rain.

When you use a series of adjectives to describe or modify a noun, you sometimes need to separate them with commas.

▶ Use commas if you could rearrange the adjectives without changing the meaning or if you could separate the adjectives with "and." Notice that all three versions of this sentence makes sense, and the versions all have essentially the same meaning.

We chose San Francisco for the conference because it is an exciting, beautiful, friendly city.

We chose San Francisco for the conference because it is a beautiful, friendly, exciting city.

We chose San Francisco for the conference because it is an exciting and beautiful and friendly city.

▶ If you are using a series of adjectives and only some of them can be rearranged without changing the meaning, use commas only around those that can be rearranged.

We need four clear, professional, glossy black-and-white photographs by March 10.

Sally and Winnie were lucky to have balcony, front-row center seats for the opera.

We hope to renovate the unique, historic nineteenth century hotel instead of building a new one.

▶ Using a comma between adjectives that do not modify the noun separately. These are the descriptive words that can't be rearranged or joined with "and."

Wrong The firm is hiring five, young, computer-literate graduates to work in the marketing department.

Wrong The firm is hiring young five computer-literate graduates to work in the marketing department.

Wrong The firm is hiring five and young and computer-literate graduates to work in the marketing department.

Right The firm is hiring five young computer-literate graduates to work in the marketing department.

▶ Using a comma to separate the final adjective from the noun it describes.

Wrong The agents asked for a colorful, interesting, meaningful, presentation.

Right The agents asked for a colorful, interesting, meaningful presentation.

Examples

Wrong   Violet is a hard-working responsible sensitive assistant.

Right   Violet is a hard-working, responsible, sensitive assistant.

Wrong   Sutpen and Company moved into spacious, light well-designed offices.

Right   Sutpen and Company moved into spacious, light, well-designed offices.

Wrong   Kay asked the caterer to serve cold, roast, chicken at the conference lunch.

Right   Kay asked the caterer to serve cold roast chicken at the conference lunch.

Wrong   The staff was asked to produce a clear concise, accurate, report.

Right   The staff was asked to produce a clear, concise, accurate report.

Wrong	Do not purchase cheap, used, oak desks.
Right	Do not purchase cheap used oak desks.
Wrong	I would suggest that you stop wearing that torn, ugly, silk, jacket to work.
Right	I would suggest that you stop wearing that torn, ugly silk jacket to work.

. . . it is a sound principle that as few stops should be used as will do the work . . .

THE KING'S ENGLISH, 1930.

Use Commas to Set Off Direct Quotations

Think About It

Quotation marks are most commonly used around direct quotations and the titles of articles, short stories, poems, songs, and some other published works. Quotation marks are also used for other purposes, such as to enclose sayings, highlight information, and indicate irony.

Here are the guidelines.

▶ Use a comma to introduce the words someone actually spoke or wrote.

Page 54 of the operating manual clearly states, "Photocopy the first and last pages of each document you send."

The moderator said, "I'm sure that most of you have heard about the time that Miquel Herman broke all the math records at this school."

▶ If the sentence continues after the direct quotation ends, place a comma *inside* the final quotation marks to separate the quote from the rest of the sentence.

Although Ms. Kelly testified, "On the night of the murder⊙ I was at home watching my favorite television programs," a neighbor stated that he saw her enter the house at midnight.

"Our business is helping you build your successful business," exclaimed the promotional brochure.

▶ When using quotes to name an article or other published work, use a comma before the first quotation marks. Also use a comma *inside* the final quotation marks if the sentence continues.

See Kantor's article, "Renewing the Work Force," published in last month's association journal.

▶ Omit the commas when using the word "in" to introduce the title of a published work.

I found the ideas Kantor expressed in "Renewing the Work Force" extremely interesting.

► Use a comma when quoting familiar sayings, and use a comma inside the final quote marks if the sentence continues.

Wrong   Whenever I begin something new, I consider the suggestion, "Look before you leap", which was one of my father's favorite sayings.

Right   Whenever I begin something new, I consider the suggestion, "Look before you leap," which was one of my father's favorite sayings.

► When using quote marks, leave the commas out if the quoted words would not ordinarily be set off with commas.

When taking exams, it's always hard to say for sure that something is "true" or "false."

After falling on the ice, Joe didn't know whether to laugh or cry when he was told to "have a nice day."

▶ Placing the comma outside the final quotation marks. When a sentence continues beyond the quoted material, always put the comma *inside* the final quote marks.

<u>Wrong</u>   "Don't think too much about the meaning of the new campaign", Jake told the assembled group.

<u>Right</u>   "Don't think too much about the meaning of the new campaign," Jake told the assembled group.

▶ Using only the first comma and leaving out the comma before the final quotation marks.

<u>Wrong</u>   My grandfather liked to say, "Don't burn your bridges" and until I was ten I thought he meant it literally.

<u>Right</u>   My grandfather liked to say, "Don't burn your bridges," and until I was ten I thought he meant it literally.

▶ Using a comma before or after quoted words if you would not use a comma if there were no quotation marks.

Wrong   My brother reads, "Travel Tips," in the newspaper every Sunday even though he never leaves home.

Right   My brother reads "Travel Tips" in the newspaper every Sunday even though he never leaves home.

Wrong "This is the most astonishing breakthrough in cell development in this century", Wendie told the group.

Right "This is the most astonishing breakthrough in cell development in this century," Wendie told the group.

Wrong Suki reported "I think the project should be canceled," and left the room where everyone sat in amazed silence.

Right Suki reported, "I think the project should be canceled," and left the room where everyone sat in amazed silence.

Wrong "I don't need to change the way things are done in this organization" the CEO stated in his opening remarks.

Right "I don't need to change the way things are done in this organization," the CEO stated in his opening remarks.

Wrong   Of all the poems he'd ever read, Bennie loved **,** "The Ancient Mariner **,** " the most.

Right   Of all the poems he'd ever read **,** Bennie loved "The Ancient Mariner" the most.

Wrong   My daughter tells me that the noise coming from her bedroom is **,** "music."

Right   My daughter tells me that the noise coming from her bedroom is "music."

People who use commas correctly write the way Michael Jordan plays basketball —all smoothness and grace with nothing left to chance.

AARON CHAN

Rule 8

USE COMMAS TO SEPARATE THE PARTS OF DATES, ADDRESSES, AND NUMBERS

 *Think About It*

Commas are used to separate the parts of dates, addresses, and large numbers so they are easier to read. Notice how much easier it is to sort out the individual elements when commas are used.

Wrong   I moved to 1105 Fifth Avenue Chicago Illinois on May 5 1999 and I have never regretted the decision.

Right   I moved to 1105 Fifth Avenue, Chicago, Illinois, on May 5, 1999, and I have never regretted the decision.

Wrong   We estimate that the improvements to the community house will cost approximately $100600 and will be completed by February 1 2002 unless we find serious probelms in the structure.

Right   We estimate that the improvements to the community house will cost approximately $100,600 and will be completed by February 1, 2002, unless we find serious problems in the structure.

Here are the guidelines.

Dates

▶ If the date contains a day, use a comma to separate the day from the year.

Our company opened for business on August 30, 1999.

▶ Use a comma after the year when another idea follows.

We plan to begin construction on August 15, 2002, depending on the results of the environmental impact report.

▶ If you wish, you can omit the comma after the year if the next part of the sentence continues the thought and you're sure that leaving the comma out won't cause confusion.

We began construction on April 28, 1997 and finished two years later.

▶ When the date does not contain a day, you do not need a comma between the month and the year, although the comma would not be wrong.

March 1999 was a very windy month.

March, 1999 was a very windy month.

Addresses

▶ Use commas between the street and city, and between the city and state. You do not need a comma between the state and the zip code.

She sent the bill to 410 Oak Drive, San Anselmo, California 94960.

▶ When using a state postal code instead of writing out the name of the state, you do not need commas between the city or town and postal code, but either way is correct.

She sent the bill to 410 Oak Drive, San Anselmo, CA 94960.

She sent the bill to 410 Oak Drive, San Anselmo CA 94960.

▶ Use commas to separate names, titles, suite numbers, apartment numbers, etc., from the rest of the address.

My editor's new mailing address is Sonia Wilson, Senior Editor, Blue Sun Publishing, 1445 Bolinas Street, Suite 6A, Fairfax, CA 94930.

Numbers

▶ Use a comma to separate the parts of numbers that have more than four digits. Starting from the right, separate the digits into groups of three. The comma is optional in four-digit groups.

The airline miles reward program now requires 25,000 miles for a free domestic flight.

The property consists of 9,670 acres of mountains, forests, and meadows.

▶ Do not use commas to separate groups of numbers used for addresses, dates, or zip codes, even when they are more than four digits long.

Wrong The package was delivered by mistake to 11,006 Eliseo instead of 1006 Eliseo.

Right The package was delivered by mistake to 11006 Eliseo instead of 1006 Eliseo.

Optional commas have been circled.

Wrong   We sent the application to George Madson, 3621 Elm Ave. Tulsa Oklahoma, one month before the policy expired on February 1, 1999.

Right   We sent the application to George Madson, 3621 Elm Ave., Tulsa, Oklahoma, one month before the policy expired on February 1, 1999.

Wrong   Please send the proposal to me at 4763, Magnolia Avenue, Los Angeles, California, 97322.

Right   Please send the proposal to me at 4763 Magnolia Avenue, Los Angeles, California 97322.

Wrong   The homes will cost upwards of $500000, and the developers plan to cut down more than 2200 trees.

Right   The homes will cost upwards of $500,000ⓐand the developers plan to cut down more than 2ⓐ200 trees.

Wrong   In June 1999 our headquarters moved to 401, Second Street, W. 3rd Floor, Newark, CA, 70132.

Right   In Juneⓐ1999ⓐour headquarters moved to 401 Second Street W., 3rd Floor, Newarkⓐ CA 70132.

Today, magazines and newspapers employ about half as many punctuation marks as they did fifty years ago. Sentences are much shorter and language has progressed toward simplicity.

ENGLISH THE EASY WAY, 1996

Rule 9

USE COMMAS TO SET OFF OTHER PUNCTUATION MARKS

 *Think About It*

Rule 7 explains how to use commas with quotation marks. This rule provides guidelines for using commas correctly with some of the other punctuation marks: periods used with abbreviations, parentheses, and semicolons.

Periods Used with Abbreviations

▶ When commas are needed to set off abbreviations, put the final comma *after* the period.

Diana Poser, M.D., will be the keynote speaker at our annual conference.

The season's first production opens on October 12 at 8:30 p.m., and you can pick up your tickets after 6:00 that evening.

Parentheses

▶ Use a comma after the *final* mark if you would use a comma without the parentheses.

I plan to take all my vacation time at once (if my manager agrees), although I still have not chosen the specific dates.

The community college is building a new computer lab (due to open next March), and it will be three times as large as the old one.

Semicolons

▶ You can use semicolons to separate items in a series and to replace the commas and coordinating conjunctions that join two closely related independent clauses.

Although you might use commas in the rest of the sentence, do not use a comma immediately before or after the semicolon.

When planting bulbs, you might mass a single variety in a handsome pot; tulips and daffodils look especially pretty this way.

Common Comma Blunder

▶ Using a comma before the first parenthesis. Never use a comma before the first mark, even if you would use a comma at that spot without the parentheses.

Wrong   I enjoy reading good travel writers, (such as Jan Morris), because it's almost like visiting the places they describe.

Right   I enjoy reading good travel writers (such as Jan Morris) because it's almost like visiting the places they describe.

Examples

Wrong   The seminar meets every Thursday evening, 7 p.m., to 9 p.m., beginning Oct., 8 and concluding Dec., 6.

Right   The seminar meets every Thursday evening, 7 p.m. to 9 p.m., beginning Oct. 8 and concluding Dec. 6.

Wrong   Allison Rose R.N., has been nominated to sit on the board of the community hospital.

Right   Allison Rose, R.N., has been nominated to sit on the board of the community hospital.

Wrong   Small-cap mutual funds are those investing in companies with market capitalization typically under $1 billion, (according to Morningstar).

Right   Small-cap mutual funds are those investing in companies with market capitalization typically under $1 billion (according to Morningstar).

Right   Aging gracefully requires a positive attitude; it also requires good health and money in the bank.

Instructors and writers of text books (impressive as is the evidence to the contrary) are human and do not invent rules to puzzle you. They do not, in fact, invent rules at all, but only make convenient applications of principles which generations of writers have found to be wisest and best.

CENTURY HANDBOOK OF WRITING, 1918

Insert commas as needed in these sentences.

1. Jackson told his co-workers that he would quit if he didn't get a promotion.

2. Anna quoted George Lehman who said "We must always stop to consider the feelings of our clients"; then she asked everyone to report on one key conversation.

3. "It's not enough to be Number Three in the industry so we must find ways to become Number One" the CEO announced at the shareholders' meeting.

4. Our V. P. of Operations announced the decision to relocate the company to New Mexico where there is a large supply of well-trained ambitious computer engineers.

5. He described an accident that had happened on July 4 1998.

6. We hope you can find us a bright centrally located inexpensive apartment.

7. Until May 2002 you can forward my mail to 374 Clarke St. San Francisco CA 94113.

8. Until she left for college Margie had never lived in a town with more than 8000 people.

9. Because she had been driving over 80 m.p.h. Anita was not surprised to see a highway patrol light flashing in her rear view mirror.

10. The building was purchased for $796400 on August 3 1996 by an investment group that listed its address as P.O. Box 73 Phoenix Arizona 85014 but a letter we sent to that address was returned.

The optional commas are circled. If you missed any, review the pages shown in parentheses.

1. Jackson told his co-workers that he would quit if he didn't get a promotion. *(Page 63)*

2. Anna quoted George Lehman who said, "We must always stop to consider the feelings of our clients"; then she asked everyone to report on one key conversation. *(Pages 59 and 74)*

3. "It's not enough to be Number Three in the industry⊙so we must find ways to become Number One," the CEO announced at the shareholders' meeting. *(Pages 18 and 60)*

4. Our V. P. of Operations announced the decision to relocate the company to New Mexico⊙where there is a large supply of well-trained, ambitious computer engineers. *(Pages 32 and 54)*

5. He described an accident that had happened on July 4, 1998. *(Page 68)*

6. We hope you can find us a bright, centrally located, inexpensive apartment. *(Page 53)*

7. Until May 2002, you can forward my mail to 374 Clarke St., San Francisco, CA 94113. *(Pages 68, 69, and 73)*

8. Until she left for college, Margie had never lived in a town with more than 8,000 people. *(Pages 28 and 70)*

9. Because she had been driving over 80 m.p.h., Anita was not surprised to see a highway patrol light flashing in her rear view mirror. *(Pages 28 and 73)*

10. The building was purchased for $796,400 on August 3, 1996, by an investment group that listed its address as P.O. Box 73, Phoenix, Arizona 85014, but a letter we sent to that address was returned. *(Pages 68, 69, and 70)*

Try It One More Time

Here are three practice exercises to help you pull together the comma rules you reviewed in this book.

The entrance to the cave is only a narrow fissure in the rock but it widens into a large cavern with a back entrance. Inside the air is cool and sound is distorted. Oystercatchers dart above our heads their flapping wings echoing like snapping towels in a strong wind. We ride the roller coaster of kayaks bumping amiably in the close quarters. When told we're about to leave the cave I start my approach grazing the rocks and turning out just as a large set of swells hits. But the real ride comes as I'm paddling back to the beach. In a stroke of luck I catch a huge curl and shoot wildly toward the shore. However a wave catches my kayak and dumps me face-first into the water.

▲　▲　▲

When we revised our human resource policies in June 1999 our objective was to encourage personal excellence through interaction communication and support not to spell out every detail. Thus the policies included in this handbook are guidelines not directives. As our President stated in her message to the company (at the conference in San Diego California on October 2 1999) "I expect all of our employees to use common sense and show common courtesy in their dealings with colleagues and customers alike."

▲　▲　▲

When the original IBM PC was designed back in 1984 the engineers were obviously not thinking about the next millennium. The problem was that most older personal computers could not interpret the change of century because the real-time clock (the memory chip that holds the date setting) had only two digits in which to store the year. As a result when Jan. 1 2000 rolled around the clock would reset itself to Jan. 1 1900. Then the computer interpreting that year as invalid would reset the clock again this time to March 1 1980 the first valid date as far as the computer was concerned.

Answers are on the next page.

 *Answers*

The optional commas are circled.

The entrance to the cave is only a narrow fissure in the rock(,)but it widens into a large cavern with a back entrance. Inside, the air is cool and sound is distorted. Oystercatchers dart above our heads, their flapping wings echoing like snapping towels in a strong wind. We ride the roller coaster of kayaks bumping amiably in the close quarters. When told we're about to leave the cave(,) I start my approach, grazing the rocks and turning out just as a large set of swells hits. But the real ride comes as I'm paddling back to the beach. In a stroke of luck(,) I catch a huge curl and shoot wildly toward the shore. However, a wave catches my kayak and dumps me face-first into the water.

▲ ▲ ▲

When we revised our human resource policies in June(,) 1999(,)our objective was to encourage personal excellence through interaction, communication(,)and support, not to spell out every detail. Thus, the policies included in this handbook are guidelines, not directives. As our President stated in her message to the company (at the conference in San Diego, California, on October 2, 1999), "I expect all of our employees to use common sense and show common courtesy in their dealings with colleagues and customers alike."

▲   ▲   ▲

When the original IBM PC was designed back in 1984, the engineers were obviously not thinking about the next millennium. The problem was that most older personal computers could not interpret the change of century because the real-time clock (the memory chip that holds the date setting) had only two digits in which to store the year. As a result, when Jan. 1, 2000, rolled around, the clock would reset itself to Jan. 1, 1900. Then the computer, interpreting that year as invalid, would reset the clock again, this time to March 1, 1980, the first valid date as far as the computer was concerned.

Suggested Reading

How To Be Your Own Best Editor, Bary Tarsish, Three Rivers Press. Explains the nuts and bolts of self-editing and suggests simple tools to make everything you write clear and concise.

Rewrite Write, Jan Venolia, Ten Speed Press. A handy guide to the process of reviewing and rewriting your work.

The Deluxe Transitive Vampire (The Ultimate Handbook of Grammar for the Innocent, The Eager, and the Doomed), Karen Elizabeth Gordon, Pantheon Books. An entertaining guide that explains rules and uses humor to make intricate and impossible usages clear.

The Elements of Style, William Strunk, Jr. and E.B. White, MacMillan Company. Includes rules of usage, principles of composition, and a list of commonly misused words and expressions.

Writing Down the Bones: Freeing the Writer Within, Natalie Goldberg, Shambhala Publications, Inc. Thoughts, suggestions, encouragement, and exercises that help free your creativity and allow your ideas to flow unencumbered onto the page.

Writing With Power: Techniques for Mastering the Writing Process, Peter Elbow. Oxford University Press. Method for getting power over yourself and over the writing process by knowing what you really mean and writing convincingly.

Other Books Published by Advanced Communication Designs

Grammar for Grownups
This self-paced training program provides pointers for improving sentence structure, explains how to use punctuation marks, and clarifies commonly confused words.

Professional Writing Skills
Written in a self-paced format, this book provides a step-by-step process for planning E-mails, letters, memos, and other documents. It also explains how to write clear, effective openings, transitions and closings; use concise, active language; and avoid gender bias.

Writing Performance Documentation
This self-paced book is a mini-course on how to describe performance clearly and objectively and write performance objectives that clearly describe what a person will do to meet job requirements. The book includes examples, practice exercises, and feedback.

How to Write Reports and Proposals
This self-paced course provides a practical process for clarifying readers' most important questions, identifying report sections, and addressing the needs of readers with different backgrounds. It also includes guidelines for using lists and visuals, and for using language that communicates clearly.

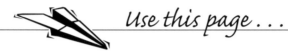 *Use this page...*

... to write down your questions about the use of commas. When you have gathered several questions, send them to us at the mail, fax, or E-mail address in the front of the book. We'll do our best to answer your questions.

_____

_____

_____

_____

_____

_____

_____

_____

_____

_____

_____

_____

_____

_____

_____

. . . to write down sentences in which you think the misuse of commas confuses readers or changes the meaning. When you have gathered several sentences, send them to us. If we use one or more of your sentences on our web page, we'll send you a free book.

_____

_____

_____

_____

_____

_____

_____

_____

_____

_____

_____

_____

_____

_____

_____

_____

_____

_____

Use these pages . . .

. . . to add your own notes about the use of commas.

_____

_____

_____

_____

_____

_____

_____

_____

_____

_____

_____

_____

_____

_____

_____

_____

_____

_____

_____

_____

_____

_____

_____